영어재미붙이기

어원과 동사

김준우 저

전남대학교출판문화원

이명혜 마리아 막달레나 靈前에 이 책을 바칩니다.

One Art

Elizabeth Bishop

The art of losing isn't hard to master;
so many things seem filled with the intent
to be lost that their loss is no disaster.

Lose something every day.
Accept the fluster of lost door keys,
the hour badly spent.
The art of losing isn't hard to master.

Then practice losing farther,
losing faster: places, and names,
and where it was you meant to travel.
None of these will bring disaster.

...

--Even losing you (the joking voice, a gesture I love)
I shan't have lied.
It's evident the art of losing's not too hard to master
though it may look like (Write it!) like disaster.

서문

쓰다 보니 쉬운 책이 손에 잡혀 있다. 어원과 동사 두 가지를 다루고 있다.

어려운 단어일수록 쉽게 해주기에, 어원은 중요하다. 이 책과 더불어, 『어원 + 어원 = 영단어』 <김준우 저> 부록 '앞에 붙는 어원'을 살펴보기 권한다.

다른 책과 달리, 명쾌한 어원만 다룬다. 그림 뿐 아니라 충분한 예문을 제시해 완벽 이해를 꾀한다.

pel = push

pro<forward> + pel<push> = propel

All of the things that have happened in my life have been self-propelled.

여기에 동사를 추가한다. 예를 들어보자. set, put, lay 셋은 다른 느낌으로 무엇을 둔다. 두어서 째깍째깍 작동시키고, 툭 놔두고, 조심스럽게 살짝 둔다.

그래서 set off, put off, lay off 세 가지가 각각 다른 의미를 가지게 되는 것이다.

학업 취업 둘 다 기본 단어가 중요하다. TOEFL 경우가 대표적이다. 쉬워 보이는데도 힘든 건, 정확한 이해가 없어서이다.

어머니 간병해주신 이무순 이모와 기도해주신 최상준 유스티노 신부님이, 먼저 생각난다. 구진만, 김중모, 박재영, 신현덕, 안준모, 유영준, 정우철, 정유인에게 고마움을 전한다. MSU 유학 시절 안병국 김동근 두 학형에게도 그러하다. 늘 이야기 들어주시는 박상훈 선생님에게 감사드린다. 고대 사회학과 박길성 교수님은 뵐 때마다 힘이 되어 주셨다. 같이 공부한 전남대 학생들은, 공저자이다.

원고를 봐 주신 송미숙 선생님, 표지를 만들어 주신 배광현 선생님, 과정을 진행해 주신 박상협 선생님이 손으로 만질 수 있게 책을 만들어 주셨다.

2022년

저자

차례

1

앞으로 pro 미는 pel 프로펠러 propeller

pro(forward) + pel(push) = propel

- 배나 비행기를 앞으로 밀면 propeller [prəpélər][1]

- 앞 밀다 → propel [prəpél] 앞으로 나아가게 하다
- moment [móumənt] 순간, misery [mízəri] 비참함
- chain [ʧein] 체인을 감다, blame [bleim] ~을 탓하다

The power of just ONE moment can propel you to success and happiness or chain you to failure and misery. - Steve Maraboli

1) https://ac-illust.com/clip-art/1651826/----

All of the things that have happened in my life have been self-propelled. I can't blame anybody else or point a finger at anybody. - Shia LaBeouf

re(back) + pel(push) = repel

- 뒤 밀다 → repel [ripél] 밀어내다

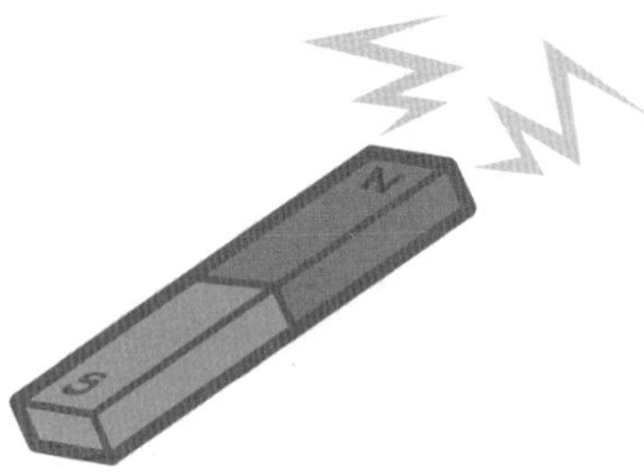

- 끌다 draw → train 기차, tractor 트랙터
- at<to> + tract<draw> = attract[ətrǽkt] 끌다
- ex<out of> + tract<draw> = extract[ikstrǽkt]추출하다
- sub<from below>+tract<draw>=subtract[səbtrǽkt] 빼다
- magnet [mǽgnit] 자석

Memory is a storm I can’t repel. - Dilys Laing

Magnets attract and repel each other.

- repellent [ripélənt] = 벌레 퇴치제[2], 뒤로 물러나게 하는

---

2) https://ac-illust.com/clip-art/1522626/

■ mosquito [məskíːtou] 모기

Mosquito repellents don't repel, they hide you. The spray blocks the mosquito's sensors so they don't know you are there.

If wealth is a magnet, poverty is a kind of repellent. - Nelson Mandela

The purity of intention repels fear. - Toba Beta

ex(out) + pel(push) = expel

■ 바깥 밀다 → expel[ikspél] 내쫓다[3], 퇴학시키다
■ sanction [sǽŋkʃən] 제재, tie [tai] 관계

In 1995, sanctions led Sudan to cut its ties with terrorists and expel Osama bin Laden.

3) https://ac-illust.com/clip-art/22265237/

We must expel Arabs and take their place. - David Ben Gurion

I don't much mind being expelled from communities. - Tony Judt

I was expelled from four schools. Today I still read with difficulty. - Sarah Miles

com(together) + pel(push) = compel

- 같이 밀다 → compel [kəmpél] 무엇을 하도록 강제하다
- ad <toward> + vise <see> = advise [ədváiz] 충고하다
- invite[inváit] 초대하다, cruelty[krú：əlti] 잔인함

To advise is not to compel. - Anton Chekhov

God's presence is not just Light, and Life, but Love.

And Love invites, but does not compel. - Frederica Mathewes-Green

Love compels cruelty To those who do not understand love. - T. S. Eliot

im(into) + pel(push) = impel

- 안으로 밀다 → impel [kəmpél] ~을 하도록 하다
- compel 보다 강제 느낌 작은 것이 impel

To teach is to touch the heart and impel it to action. - Louis Sullivan

Every suffering is a seed, because suffering impels us to seek wisdom. - Bodhidharma

While early childhood experiences may impel, they do not compel. In the end, evil is a matter of choice. - Andrew Vachss

dis(away from) + pel(push) = dispel

- 산산이 흩어지게 밀다 → dispel[dispél] 싹 없애버리다

Only love dispels hate. - Buddha

2

정상적 normal, 초자연적 paranormal

- norm [nɔ : rm] 규범, normal [nɔ́ : rməl] 정상적
- normalize [nɔ́ : rməlàiz] 정상화하다.
- im<into>+ply<fasten 동여매다> = imply[implái] 암시하다
- ap<to>+ply<fasten[fǽsn]> = apply[əplái] 적용하다

Originality implies being bold enough to go beyond accepted norms. - Anthony Storr

Everyone is normal until you get to know them.

As long as Fidel Castro is alive we will not normalize relations with Cuba. - Mark Falcoff

para(beyond) + normal(rule) = paranormal

■ paranormal [perənɔ́ : rməl] = 초자연적[1)]

But I do believe in the paranormal, that there are things our brains just can't understand. - Art Bell

ab(off, away from) + normal(rule) = abnormal

■ 멀어지다 정상[2)] → abnormal [æbnɔ́ : rməl] 비정상

Abnormal is so common, it's practically normal.

e(out of) + normous(rule) = enormous

■ 벗어나다 기준 → enormous [inɔ́ : rməs] 엄청난
■ 길이, 무게, 크기에 사용 가능하다. 비유적으로도 쓰인다.
■ tongue[tʌŋ] 혀, ape[eip] 영장류, span[spæn] 뻗치다.

So also the tongue is a small thing, but what enormous damage it can do. - James 3:5

Gorillas are the largest of the great apes. A mature male may be six feet tall and weigh 400 pounds or more; his enormous arms can span eight feet.

---

1) https://ac-illust.com/clip-art/2202990/cosmic-man
2) https://www.etymonline.com/

3

grow → 크루아상 croissant, 초승달 crescent

■ croissant[krəsɑ́ː nt] 초승달 모양 빵 크루아상[1]

■ crescent[krésnt] 초승달

■ 새로 차오르는 달 = 初生달 = (오른쪽이 둥근) 초승달

■ Fertile Crescent = 비옥한 초승달 지대 (이집트~이라크)

The Tigris and Euphrates Rivers created the 'Fertile Crescent' where some of the first civilizations emerged. - Stephen Kinzer

1) https://ac-illust.com/clip-art/22343235/

- civil [sívəl] 예의바른, civilization [sìvəlaizéiʃən] 문명
- fertile [fə́ ː rtail] 비옥한
- e<out of> + merge<dip> = 떠오르다 emerge [imə́ ː rdʒ]
- sub<under>+merge=submerge[səbmə́ ː rdʒ] 물에 잠기다

Some submarines can stay submerged indefinitely.

But I would rather be with you, somewhere in San Francisco on a back porch in July, just looking up to Heaven, at this crescent in the sky - Robert Hunter

- crescendo [kriʃéndou] (음악용어) 점점 세게[2)]

표기	이탈리아어	뜻
cresc. <	크레센도	점점 세게
decresc. dim. >	데크레센도, 디미누엔도	점점 약하게

크레센도와 데크레센도의 보표예

- wave[weiv] 파도, ~몇 차
- Europe is facing a third-wave of Covid-19.

Love is a wave building to a crescendo. Ride if you will, ride it with me. - Jimmy Buffett

---

2) https://ko.wikipedia.org/wiki/셈여림표

- 자라다, 커지다 grow → 보충 부대[3] → crew[kru：] 선원[4]

ac(to) + crue(grow) = accrue

- accrue [əkrú：] = (증가해서) 생기다
- port [pɔ：rt] 항구 → importance [impɔ́：rtəns] 중요

Vacation time is something we all accrue, but only the wisest of us recognize its importance.

- affect[əfékt] 영향을 미치다 = af<to> + fect<do>
- effect[ifékt] 영향 = ef<out> + fect<do>

How we treat people and affect their lives for the good is the true wealth that we accrue in life.

re(again) + cruit(grow) = recruit

3) Oxford Languages
4) https://ac-illust.com/clip-art/797123/ship--with-people-

■ recruit [rikrú : t] = (군인, 직원을) 모으다

Recruiting is hard. - Steve Jobs

Saudi Arabia opens military recruitment to women.[5)]

in(into) + crease(grow) = increase

■ increase [inkrí : s] = 늘어나다, 명사 increase [ínkri : s]

■ cor<together> + rupt<break> = corrupt[kərʌpt] 부패한

■ feed[fi : d] 먹이다, 공급하다. feed-fed-fed

Man is the only animal whose desires increase as they are fed; the only animal that is never satisfied.

Corruption is like a ball of snow, once it's set a rolling it must increase. - Charles Caleb Colton

de(down) + crease(grow) = decrease

■ decrease [dikrí : s] = 줄어들다, 명사 decrease [dí : kri : s]

Your value does not decrease based on someone's inability to see your worth. - Zig Ziglar

---

5) Gulf Business, by Zainab Mansoor.February 21, 2021

④ script, Scripture, manuscript, describe

- 쓰다 write → script [skript] 문자, 글씨체, 대본[1]
- P.S. = Post Script = 편지를 다 쓰고 덧붙이는 글

```
                                                          11.

                    JOHN
          Well, one can't have everything.

                                                     CUT TO:

EXT. JOHN AND MARY'S HOUSE - CONTINUOUS

An old car pulls up to the curb and a few KNOCKS as the
engine shuts down.

MIKE steps out of the car and walks up to the front door. He
rings the doorbell.

                                                    BACK TO:

INT. KITCHEN - CONTINUOUS

                    JOHN
          Who on Earth could that be?

                    MARY
          I'll go and see.
```

- make sense = 말이 되다, define [difáin] 규정하다

1) wikipedia commons Screenplay_example.svg

You define your own life. Don't let other people write your script. - Oprah Winfrey

The difference between life and the movies is that a script has to make sense, and life doesn't. - Joseph L. Mankiewicz

To make a great film you need three things - the script, the script and the script. Alfred Hitchcocke

■ hieroglyphic [hàiərəglífik] script 그림문자[2)]

2) wikimedia commons Ebony plaque of Menes in his tomb of Abydos

■ hieroglyph[háiərəglìf] 그림문자, carving[kɑ́ : rviŋ] 조각
■ literally [lítərəli] 말 그대로, sacred [séikrid] 성스러운

Hieroglyphic script is the first script used by the ancient Egyptians to write their language. The word hieroglyph literally means "sacred carvings".

■ 쓰다 write → Scripture [skríptʃər] 성경[3]
■ scriptures 어떤 한 종교의 경전, Hindu scriptures[4]

The devil can cite Scripture for his purpose. - William Shakespeare, The Merchant of Venice

manu(hand) + script(write) = manuscript

■ manuscript [mǽnjuskrìpt] 손으로 쓴 것, 원고

---

3) https://ac-illust.com/clip-art/2222854/
4) Oxford Advanced Learner's Dictionary

When you write a manuscript, it feels like being in a relationship with someone. You'll hate it, get bored with it, be pissed of, like you just want to break up. But, just like any relationship, you will fall in love again and again, like you don't want to lose it. - Alvi Syahri

- manual [mǽnjuəl] 손으로 하는
- manual labor 손으로 하는 일, 힘든 육체 노동

  Manual labor can be tough on your body.

- manual transmission = 수동변속기

  It is hard to sell a car with manual transmission.

- 쓰다 write → scribble [skríbl] 휘갈겨 쓰다, 낙서하다[5)]

- mark × 표시, 점수, 자국, 표시, 과녁, 중요성
- make a mark 중요한 성취를 이루다

5) https://ac-illust.com/ko/clip-art/226237/

- witness [wítnis] 목격하다, 목격자
- doubt [daut] 의심하다, 의심
- experience [ikspíəriəns] 경험하다, 경험

We have to make a mark, even if it's only a scribble. - John Steinbeck

When in doubt, scribble. - Jean Wilson

My sketchbook is a witness of what I am experiencing, scribbling things whenever they happen. - Vincent Van Gogh

pre(before) + scribe(write) = prescribe

- 미리 쓰다 → 방향이나 규칙을 적어두다 → 처방하다6)
- '규정하다' 의미도 있음
- law[lɔ：] 법, penalty[pénəlti] 처벌, false[fɔ：ls] 거짓
- statement[stéitmənt] 진술, provide[prəváid] 제공하다

The law prescribes a maximum penalty of 3 years in prison for providing a false statement.

It's always dangerous to prescribe an idea on other people. - Tom Sturridge

---

6) https://www.etymonline.com/word/prescribe

- prescription [priskrípʃən] 처방전
- prescription drug 처방전 있어야 하는 약
- over-the-counter drug 일반의약품
  (계산대 counter 넘어 over 그냥 사는 약)
- OTC drug 일반의약품, OTC stock 장외주식
- antibiotics[æntibaiάtik]항생제, pharmacy[fά : rməsi]약국

In most developing countries, you can buy antibiotics over-the-counter at pharmacies or even at grocery stores.

- believe in ~이 좋다고 믿다, ~의 존재를 믿다
- bill [bil] 계산서, 지폐, 법안 neat [ni : t] 깔끔한

I believe in prescription drugs. I believe in feeling better. - Denis Leary

You may not be able to read a doctor's handwriting and prescription, but you'll notice his bills are neatly typewritten. - Earl Wilson

That's my prescription for a happy marriage - marry someone who doesn't do anything similar to what you do. - Maxine Kumin

de(down) + scribe(write) = describe

- 적어두다 write down → 형태 표시하다[7] → 묘사하다
- description[diskrípʃən]묘사, landscape[lǽndskeip]경치
- vantage[vǽntidʒ] 유리함, vantage point 전망좋은 지점
- diminish[dimíniʃ] 작게 하다

Life is like a landscape. You live in the midst of it but can describe it only from the vantage point of distance. - Charles Lindbergh

To describe happiness is to diminish it. - Stendhal

People ask me to describe myself, but it's a very personal thing. You don't feel comfortable.

con(together) + scribe(write) = conscribe

- 같이 (이름을) 적다 → 징집하다
- conscription[kənskrípʃən] = 징병
- just[dʒʌst] 공정한, require[rikwáiər] 필요로 하다
- plentiful [pléntifəl] 충분하다
- volunteer [vὰləntíər] 자원하다

A "just war" - if there could be such a thing - would not require conscription. Volunteers would be plentiful. - Ben Salmon

7) https://www.etymonline.com/word/describe

sub(under) + scribe(write) = subscribe

- (문서) 밑 (이름) 적다 → 동의하다, 기부하다, 구독하다
- subscription [səbskrípʃən] 구독
- slave [sleiv] 노예, property [prάpərti] 소유물
- asset [ǽset] 자산, launch [lɔ：nʧ] 발사하다, 시작하다

Data has become an asset, and nobody has more customer information than a subscription business. Traditional companies are launching entire subscription offerings just for the data they provide.

I subscribe to William Faulkner's' view that history is not just about what we were before but who we are now. - Ken Burns

I do not subscribe to the doctrine that the people are the slaves and property of their government. I believe that government is for the use of the people, and not the people for the use of the government.

I subscribe to no religion. But I believe that in the creation of art, there can be moments of God. - Andrea Riseborough

circum(around) + scribe(write) = circumscribe

- [sə́ː rkəmskraib] 주위에 선 긋다, 제한하다, 범위 정하다
- circumscribed circle = circumcircle = 외접원

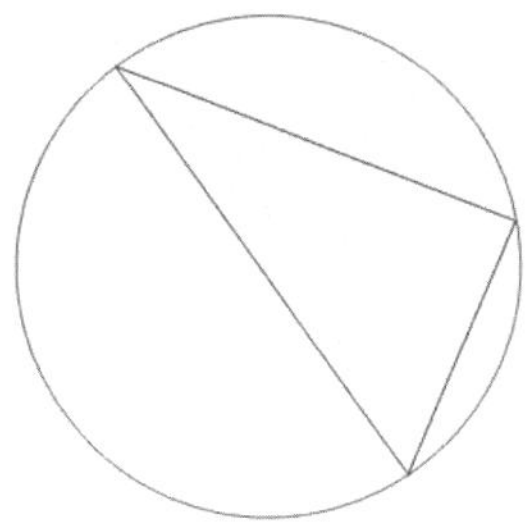

The soul circumscribes all things. - Ralph Waldo

The laws were not made so much for the direction of good men, as to circumscribe the bad.

- law[lɔː] 법, direction 방향, 지시, 지도, 지침, 감독
- good men 좋은 이, the bad 나쁜 이, soul[soul] 영혼
- di<down> + rect<put straight> = direct[dirékt][8]
- e<out> + rection<put straight> = erection 건립, 발기

a(to) + scribe(write) = ascribe

- 어느 쪽에 쓰여 있다 → ~에서 나왔다고 생각하다
- ascribed status [stéitəs] = 타고난 지위

---

8) Oxford Languages

- achieved status = 성취한 지위, achieve [əʧíːv]
- ascribe A to B = B가 A의 (원인, 탓, 공)이라 생각하다[9]

They ascribed his illness to chemicals in his brain.

Life is without meaning. You bring the meaning to it. The meaning of life is whatever you ascribe it to be. Being alive is the meaning.

- op<against>+ponent<put>=opponent [əpóunənt] 적
- motive[móutiv] 동기, mean[miːn] 비열한
- in<not> + competence<fit> = incompetence 무능
- ascribe ≈ attribute[ətríbjuːt] ~을 원인으로 여기다
- malice[mǽlis] 악의, stupidity[stjuːpídəti] 어리석음

Never ascribe to an opponent motives meaner than your own. - James M. Barrie

Never ascribe to malice that which is adequately explained by incompetence. - Napolean Bonaparte

Never attribute to malice that which is adequately explained by stupidity.

---

9) https://www.merriam-webster.com/dictionary/ascribe

5

보내다 send → mission, dismiss, submit

▪ missionary [míʃənèri] = (보내지는) 성직자[1]

▪ 보내다 → mission [míʃən] 임무, 사명

My mission in life is not merely to survive, but to thrive; and to do so with some passion, some compassion, some humor, and some style.

1) https://ac-illust.com/ko/clip-art/96354/

inter(between) + mit(to let go) = intermit

- intermit[ìntərmít] 잠시 중지하다, diet [dáiət] 식이요법
- intermission = (연극, 공연의) 막간, 휴식시간, 중지 시간
- intermittent [ìntərmítnt] = 일시적으로 멈추는, 간헐적인

Make your life a mission - not an intermission.

Intermittent fasting is not a diet. It is a pattern of eating. It does not specify what foods a person should eat or avoid.

trans(across) + mit(to let go) = transmit

- 너머 보내다 → transmit 전달하다, 전염시키다
- suffering [sΛfəriŋ] 고통
- trans<across>+form<to form>=transform 변형시키다
- in<into> + form = inform[infɔ́ : rm] 알려주다
- con<together> + form = conform[kənfɔ́ : rm] 순응하다
- re<back> + form = reform[rifɔ́ : rm] 개혁하다

If you don't transform your suffering, you will transmit it. - Richard Rohr

- transmission 전달, 엔진 힘을 바퀴로 보내는 변속기

Most people have no concept of how an automatic transmission works, yet they know how to drive a car. You don't have to study physics to understand the laws of motion to drive a car. You don't have to understand any of this stuff to use Macintosh.

Structure is more important than content in the transmission of information. - Abbie Hoffman

Art is not a handicraft, it is the transmission of feeling the artist has experienced. - Leo Tolstoy

sub(under) + mit(to let go) = submit

- 아래로 보내다 → submit[səbmít] 제출하다, 굴복하다
- discipline [dísəplin] 규율, disciple [disáipl] 성도

Whenever we submit our will to someone else's opinion, a part of us dies. - Lauryn Hill

He who submits to discipline is a DISCIPLE.

- re<again>+quire<ask>=require[rikwáiər] 요구하다
- in<into>+quire<ask>=inquire[inkwáiər] 문의하다
- welfare check 정부에서 보내는 복지 지원금 수표

I propose that every person out of work be required

to submit a book report before he or she gets his or her welfare check. - Kurt Vonnegut

com(together) + mit(to let go) = commit

- 같이 보내다 → commit [kəmít] 저지르다, ~에 전념하다

Life is an opportunity. The only crime we are committing is not taking that opportunity.

When you're committed to something, you accept no excuses - only results. - Ken Blanchard

- 잡다 catch → captive [kǽptiv] 포로
- (시선을) 잡다 catch → caption [kǽpʃən] 자막
- 잡다 catch → captivate [kǽptəvèit] 마음을 사로잡다
- ac <to> + cept <catch> = accept [æksépt] 받아들이다
- inter<between> + cept = intercept[ìntərsépt] 가로채다
- contra<against>+cept=contracept[kɔ̀ntrəsépt]피임하다
- con<together>+ceive<catch>=conceive[[kənsíːv] 임신하다, 생각하다
- re <back> + ceive <catch> = receive [risíːv] 받다
- per<through>+ceive=perceive[pərsíːv] ~로 생각하다

dis(away) + miss(to let go) = dismiss

■ 멀리 내보내다 → dismiss [dismís] 내보내다, 소송을 기각하다, 무시하다

By dismissing what could work, we dismiss our own growth. We dismiss what's possible. - Joe Vitale

Re-examine all you have been told. Dismiss that which insults your soul. - Walt Whitman

Man may dismiss compassion from his heart, but God never will. - William Cowper

com(together) + promise = compromise

■ 같이 약속 → compromise[kάmprəmàiz] 타협하다, 타협

Commitment is another name for relationship not the compromise. - Santosh Kalwar

pro(forward) + mise(to let go) = promise

■ 앞으로 보내다 → promise[prάmis] 약속하다, 약속

Don't respect someone for making a promise. Respect them for keeping it.

- re<back>+spect<look at>=respect[rispékt] 존경하다
- spectate[spékteit] 구경하다
- spectacle[spéktəkl] 구경거리
- spectator [spékteitər] 구경꾼
- spectrum [spéktrəm] (프리즘에 의한 백색광) 분광, 범위
- in<into> + spect = inspect[inspékt] 조사하다
- ex<out> + spect = expect[ikspékt] 기대하다
- sus<below> + spect = suspect[səspékt] 의심하다
- suspect [sΛspekt] 용의자
- pro<forward> + spect = prospect[prɔ́spekt] 전망
- a<to> + spect = aspect[ǽspekt] 관점, 양상
- intro<inward>+spect = introspect[ìntrə-] 자기반성하다
- retro<backward>+spect = retrospect[rétrəspèkt] 회상
- circum<around>+spect=circumspect[sə́ː rkəm-] 신중한
- de<out> + spise<look at> = despise [dispáiz] 경멸하다
- con<together> + spicuous <look at> = conspicuous [kənspíkjuəs] 과시적인

ad(to) + mit(to let go) = admit

- ~로 보내다 → admit[ədmít] 인정하다

Admit it ... life would be so boring without me.

6

만들다 make, 하다 do → factory, affect, infect

- 라틴어 facere[1)] = 만들다 make, 하다 do
- 올리브 기름 짜는 기계 oil press[2)] = factorium
- 그림에 나오는 압착기 factorium[3)] → factory

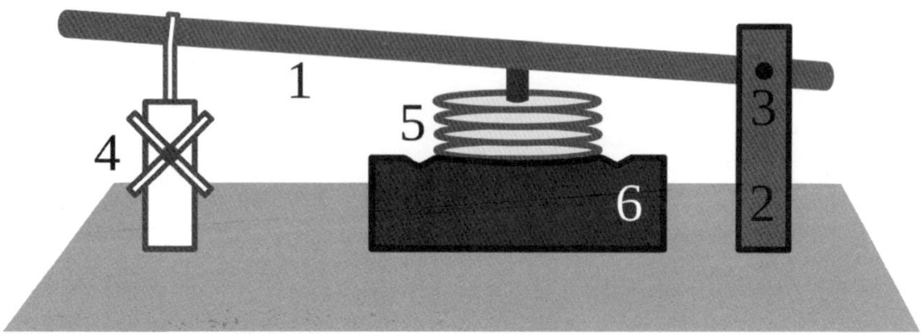

- factory [fǽktəri] = 만드는 곳 = 공장

Products are made in the factory, but brands are created in the mind. - Walter Landor

- 만들다 → feasible [fíːzəbl] 실행할 수 있는, 가능한

---

1) 라틴어 c는 [s]가 아닌 [k]로 발음. facere 에서도 마찬가지.
2) 라틴어 factorium = oil press 출처: Oxford Languages
3) commons.wikimedia.org/wiki/File:Ancient_Olive_Oil_Press.svg

It is feasible to create your own heaven on earth. - Steven Redhead

I've always made it clear that I do not believe that global government is either necessary or feasible.

- 만들다 → factor [fǽktər] 원인, 요인, 요소
- motivation [mòutəvéiʃən] 동기부여

Motivation is the single most important factor in any sort of success. - Edmund Hillary

- ad<to> + apt<to fit 맞추다> = adapt[ədǽpt] 적응하다
- sur<above> + vive<to live> = survive 생존하다

The most important factor in survival is neither intelligence nor strength but adaptability. - Charles Darwin

bene(good) + factor(do) = benefactor

- 좋은 일을 하는 → benefactor [bénəfæktər] 후원자
- charity [ʧǽrəti] 자선금, hate [heit] 미워하다

A man receiving charity always hates his benefactor - it is a fixed characteristic of human nature. George Orwell

manu(hand) + facture(make) = manufacture

- manufacture [mænjufǽkʧər] 만들다, 제조

Sometimes, you have to manufacture your own history. Give fate a push, so to speak. - Sarah Dessen

- raw[rɔ：] 가공하지 않은, obedient[oubí：diənt] 순종적인
- curious [kjúəriəs] 호기심 많은

Schooling is a manufacturing process whereby the raw material called curious boys is turned into products called obedient men. - Mokokoma Mokhonoana

- faction [fǽkʃən] = 만들어진 무리 = 당파, 파벌, 불화
- eat out of a can 통조림 음식을 먹다
- strangle [strǽŋgl] 목을 졸라 죽이다

I'd rather eat out of a can than be strangled by a faction. - Veronica Roth

arti(art) + fact(make) = artifact

- artifact [ά：rtəfækt] 사람이 만든 고고학 유물, 가공물

■ verb 동사, verbal [və́ː rbəl] 말의, solid [sɔ́lid] 단단한

Man is an artifact designed for space travel.

A poem is a verbal artifact which must be as skillfully and solidly constructed as a table or a motorcycle.

per(through) + fect(do) = perfect

- perfect[pə́ː rfikt] 완벽한, perfection[pərfékʃən] 완벽
- im<cause> + prove<profit> = improve 나아지다
- waste[weist] 쓰레기, 낭비하다 flaw[flɔː] 결점, 오류
- flake[fleik] (덩어리에서 나온) 얇은 조각, 파편 → flaw
- disaster[dizǽstər] 천재지변, 재난, 재앙, 완전한 실패
- dis<bad> + astro → aster <star> = disaster

To improve is to change; to be perfect is to change often. - Winston Churchill

We waste time looking for the perfect lover, instead of creating the perfect love. - Tom Robbins

I'm beautifully broken, perfectly imperfect, beautiful in my flaws. All together I am a beautiful disaster.

ef(out) + fect(make) = effect

- effect [ifékt] 결과, 효과
- tread[tred]발 딛다, track[træk]길 → trade[treid] 무역
- cause[kɔ：z] ~을 시키다, 원인이 되다, 원인
- cause and effect 인과관계

Peace is a natural effect of trade. - Montesquieu

Shallow men believe in luck. Strong men believe in cause and effect. - Ralph Waldo Emerson

sacri(sacred, holy) + fice(make) = sacrifice

- 성스럽게 만든 → sacrifice [sǽkrəfàis] 희생, 희생제물
- offer [ɔ́fər] 바치다

Life is a song - sing it. Life is a game - play it. Life is a challenge - meet it. Life is a dream - realize it. Life is a sacrifice - offer it. Life is love - enjoy it. - Sai Baba

arti(art) + ficial(make) = artificial

- 솜씨있게 만든 → artificial [ὰ：rtəfíʃəl] 인공적, 인위적
- AI = artificial intelligence = 인공지능

Pride makes us artificial and humility makes us real.

I don't know where the artificial stops and the real starts. - Andy Warhol

ef(out) + ficient(make) = efficient

- efficient[ifíʃənt] 효율적

Efficiency is doing things right; effectiveness is doing the right things. - Peter Drucker

suf(up to) + ficient(make) = sufficient

- 필요한 만큼 만든 → sufficient [səfíʃənt] 충분한

A very small degree of hope is sufficient to cause the birth of love. - Stendhal

Happiness belongs to the self sufficient. - Aristotle

pro(forward) + ficient(make) = proficient

- 앞서 만든 → proficient [prəfíʃənt] 능숙한
- proficiency [prəfíʃənsi] 능숙, 실력

Math proficiency is the gateway to a number of incredible careers that students may never have considered. - Danica McKellar

de(out) + ficient(make) = deficient

- 만든 것이 다 소멸한 → deficient [difíʃənt] ~이 부족한
- intro<inward>+vert<turn>=introvert [íntrəvə̀ː rt] 내향인
- snob [snab] 잘난체하는 사람
- de <down> + press <press> = depress 우울하게 하다
- racist [réisist] 인종차별주의자
- ex <out> + ceed <go> = exceed [iksíː d] 넘어서다
- excess [iksés] 초과, 넘침

When an introvert is quiet, don't assume he is depressed, snobbish or socially deficient. - Laurie Helgoe

Racists are deficient as human beings. - George C. Wolfe

Excess and deficiency are equally at fault. - Confucius

- Swiss army knife 깡통 따개 등 기능이 많은 접이식 칼

Sleep is the Swiss army knife of health. When sleep

is deficient, there is sickness and disease.

in(into) + fect(make) = infect

- infect [infékt] 감염시키다, 오염시키다, 물들이다
- 프랑스어 avant[avɑ̃]앞 → advantage[ədvǽntidʒ]유리함
- spread [spred] 엷게 바르다, 퍼트리다

Let your infectious smile infect the whole world with love and joy. - Debasish Mridha

It's the advantage of the virus to spread, and you can only spread when you infect people and they infect other people without necessarily killing them. - Anthony Fauci

af(to) + fect(do) = affect

- affect [əfékt] 영향을 주다, 작용하다, 감염시키다
- con <together> + sequence <follow> = consequence
- probable[prάbəbl]그럴듯한, probability[prὰbəbíləti]확률
- judgment 판단, judge [dʒʌdʒ] 판단하다, 재판하다, 판사

Little things affect little minds. - Benjamin Disraeli

Never hate your enemies, it affects your judgment. - The Godfather Part III (1990)

The consequences of an act affect the probability of its occurring again. - B. F. Skinner

- 달리다 run → cursor [kə́ː rsər] (컴퓨터) 커서
- ob → oc<against> + cur<run> = occur[əkə́ː r]일어나다
- in<into> + cur<run> = incur [inkə́ː r] 나쁜 무엇이 생기다

Expect little from others and you will avoid incurring resentment. - Confucius

- in<into>+cursion<run>=incursion[inkə́ː rʒən] 침입

I'd be willing to bet that any incursion throughout history in which the invading country has proclaimed it is bringing benefits to the conquered is based on a lie. - Peter Shaffer

7

앉다 sit → sedan, session, reside, possess

- 앉다 sit → sedan 앉은 채 타는 차, 세단[1]

- 앉다 sit → session [séʃən] 앉아서 하는 회의
- 앉다 sit → sedate [sidéit] 진정제를 놓다[2]

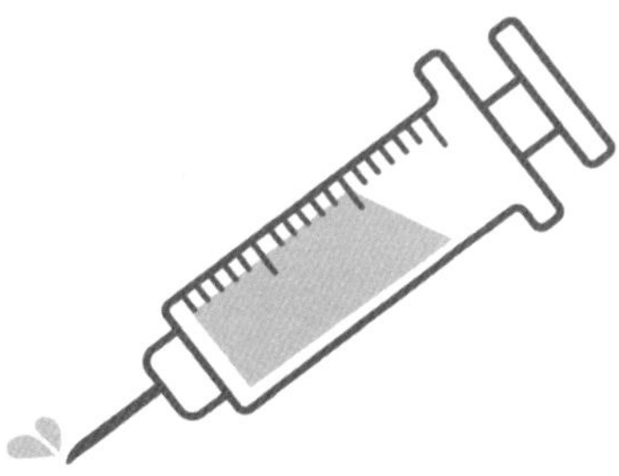

If someone is sedated, they are given a drug to calm them or to make them sleep.[3]

---

1) https://ac-illust.com/ko/clip-art/22247160
2) https://ac-illust.com/clip-art/22255810

- 앉다 sit → sediment [sédəmənt] 침전물
- sedimentary rock [sèdəméntəri][rak] 퇴적암

The finest wits have their sediment. - Ralph Waldo Emerson

pos(powerful) + sess(sit) = possess

- 강한 존재 앉다→possess[pəzés](악령에)홀리다, 소유하다
- the jeoulous 질투하는 사람, dull [dʌl] 둔한

The jealous are possessed by a mad devil and a dull spirit at the same time. - Johann Kaspar Lavater

Freedom is the sure possession of those alone who have the courage to defend it. - Pericles

pre(before) + side(sit) = preside

- 앞 앉다 → preside[prizáid]사회보다, 일을 책임지고 맡다

The director is simply the audience. His job is to pre-

3) www.collinsdictionary.com

side over accidents. - Orson Welles

re(again) + side(sit) = reside

- 또 앉아 있다 → reside [rizáid] 거주하다, 머물다
- residence[rézədəns] 거주지, paradise[pǽrədàis] 천국

If I am happy inside, then I live in paradise no matter where my residence is. - Mac Anderson

as(to) + sess(sit) = assess

- 이쪽으로 앉다 → assess [əsés] 값을 매기다, 평가하다

Courage is not the absence of fear, but rather the assessment that something else is more important than fear. - Franklin D. Roosevelt

I made my own assessment of my life, and I began to live it. That was freedom. - Fernando Flores

Assessments should compare the performance of students to a set of expectations, never to the performance of other students. - Alfie Kohn

8

서다 stand → statue, status, obstacle

- 서다 stand → statue [stǽʧuː] 동상, 조각상
- statue of liberty 자유의 여신상
- 서다 stand → stature [stǽʧər] 키, 위상

Greatness is not measured by money and stature, it is measured by courage and heart.

- steady [stédi] 안정되게, bound [baund] 뛰어오르기
- leap [liːp] 건너뛰기, leap of faith 엄청난 믿음
- leaps and bounds 일취월장 日就月將

She was small in stature and big in heart.

The body grows slowly and steadily but the soul grows by leaps and bounds. It may come to its full stature in an hour. - L.M. Montgomery

- 서다 stand → status [stéitəs] 지위, 신분
- status quo [stéitəs][kwou] 현 상태

Say it to my face, not through your status!

- 서다 stand → stable [stéibl] 안정적인

Life isn't nearly as stable as we want it to be.

- 서다 stand → state [steit] 국가

The state is made for man, not man for the state.

ob(against) + stacle(stand) = obstacle

- 마주하고 서 있는 → obstacle [ɔ́bstəkl] 방해, 장애물
- residence [rézədəns] 거주지, dwell [dwel] 거주하다
- path [pæθ] 어디로 가는 길

The obstacle is the path. - Zen proverbs

- 서다 stand → resist, persist, assist, subsist
- re<against>+sist<stand>=resist[rizíst] 저항하다
- as<to>+sist<stand>=assist[əsíst] 돕다
- per<through>+sist<stand>=persist[pərsíst] 지속하다
- sub<below>+sist<stand>=subsist[səbsíst] 근근이 살다

9

sequence → set 놔둬서 째깍째깍 작동시키다

■ sequence[síːkwəns][1] 시간에 따라 작동 → set

■ 놔두어 작동시키다 = (시계나 기계를) 설정하다 = set[2]

Happiness is ... not having to set the alarm for the next day.

■ 놔두어 작동시키다 = (목표를) 설정하다 = set[3]

Set your course by the stars, not by the lights of every passing ship. - Omar N. Bradley

■ 놔두어 작동시키다 = (기준을) 설정하다 = set

---

1) www.etymonline.com/set Old French sette "sequence"
2) https://ac-illust.com/ko/clip-art/1317475/
3) https://ac-illust.com/ko/clip-art/2656056

■ put up with 감수하다, end up with 결국 ~로 끝나다

Relationships: If you put up with it, you're going to end up with it. Set the standard you want and don't settle for less. - Steve Maraboli

If you set a good example you need not worry about setting rules. - Lee Iacocca

Setting a good example for your children takes all the fun out of middle age. - William Feather

■ 명사 setback = 일시적 실패
■ 작동하는 돈 시계를 늦추다 → set back 비용 들다

Do not allow setbacks to set you back.

The car repairs set me back five hundred dollars.

- set 놔두고 작동하다 + off 분리되어 = set off 점화하다[4]
- firecracker[fáiərkrækər]폭죽, atomic[ətámik]원자력의

A good book is enjoyable. A great book sets off a bomb inside of you. - Ned Hepburn

Other people set off firecrackers. We drop atomic bombs. - William Bourke

- set 놔두고 작동하다 + out 바깥 = set out
(여정을) 시작하다, (중요한 일을 계획 가지고) 시작하다
- order[ɔ́ : rdər] 질서, misery[mízəri] 비참함
- Mammon[mǽmən] 재물의 신 <Matthew 6,24>

When men set out to create order, they create only misery. - Marty Rubin

Those who set out to serve both God and Mammon soon discover that there is no God.

---

4) https://ac-illust.com/ko/clip-art/22230804

10

put 툭 놔두다

- put 물리적 느낌이 강해서 툭 놔두는 느낌
- input[ínpùt] = into 안쪽 + put 툭 던져두다 = 투입
- output = out 바깥쪽 + put 툭 던져두다 = 산출

Output always equals input. - James Van Fleet

- put 툭 놔두다 in 안쪽으로 → ~을 들이다

I think anything is possible if you have the mindset and the will and desire to do it and put the time in.

- put into practice 실행에 옮기다

Knowledge is of no value unless you put it into practice. - Anton Chekhov

- 툭 놔두다 + 죽음까지 → put to death 사형 집행하다

Respect me, or put me to death. - Malcolm X

- 툭 놔두다 + 위쪽으로 → put up 쌓다, 설치하다

Sometimes you put walls up not to keep people out, but to see who cares enough to break them down.

Happiness is ... putting up a Christmas tree.1)

- put up 쌓다, 설치하다 ↔ take down 해체하다, 치우다
- joyless[dʒɔ́ilis] 즐거움이 없는, cynical[sínikəl] 냉소적인

Taking down the Christmas tree makes it feel official: time to get back to joyless and cynical.

- put up 보여주다
- front [frʌnt] 앞, 정면, 겉모양

I am putting up a great front, then because I feel like I'm breaking apart inside. - Christine Feehan

- put up 보여주다 → put up a good fight 잘 싸우다

---

1) https://ac-illust.com/clip-art/22370253/

- eventually[ivénʧuəli] 결국, lose[lu：z] 지다
- hold on 계속 잡고 있다, let go 손 떼다
- acceptance[əkséptəns] 받아들임, choice[ʧɔis] 선택

Most things will be okay eventually, but not everything will be. Sometimes you'll put up a good fight and lose. Sometimes you'll hold on really hard and realize there is no choice but to let go. Acceptance is a small, quiet room. - Cheryl Strayed

- 툭 놔두다 + 위쪽 다락방에 → put up 재워주다

I can put you up for the night.

- 손을 두다 + 위쪽으로[2] → put up 상황에 대처하다
- shut up! = shut your mouth up!

Put up or shut up!

2) https://ac-illust.com/clip-art/662462/boxer

- 상황에 대처 + ~와 같이 → put up with 참다, 견디다
- reck [rek] ~을 개의하다, ~을 염려하다
- reckless [réklis] 신경을 쓰지 않는, 개의치 않는, 무모한

The way I see it, if you want the rainbow, you gotta put up with the rain. - Dolly Parton

Don't be reckless with other people's hearts. Don't put up with people who are reckless with yours.

- 툭 놔두다 + 바깥 → put out ~을 밖으로 내어놓다
- karma[kά : rmə] 업보, vibe[váib] 기운

What you put out comes back all the time, no matter what. - Oprah Winfrey

I believe in karma, and I believe if you put out positive vibes to everybody, that's all you're going to get back. - Kesha

- 툭 놔두다 + 소멸될 때까지 → put out 불 끄다

Do not light a fire that you cannot yourself put out. - Gaelic Proverbs

You can not put out fire with fire.

- 툭 놔두다 + 분리해서 → put off 미루다
- pro<forward> + mise<send> = promise[prάmis] 약속

Anger is the only thing to put off until tomorrow.

Don’t put off happiness you can have today. Tomorrow is a hope, not a promise.

- 툭 놔두다 + 아래로 → put down 내려 놓다

Put down your gun!

- 툭 놔두다 + 아래로 → put down 남 앞에서 깎아내리다

You don't build yourself up by putting someone else down. - Mitch Mitchell

- 툭 놔두다 + 아래로 → put down 쓰다

My aim is to put down on paper what I see and what I feel in the best and simplest way. - Ernest Hemingway.

- 툭 던져두다 + 옆에 → put aside 한쪽에 두다,
- set down 내려놓다, pride [praid] 자부심
- arrogance[ǽrəgəns] 오만, grave [greiv] 무덤

Put aside your pride, Set down your arrogance, And remember your grave. - Ali ibn Abi Talib

- put money aside 돈을 따로 떼어 관리하다
- save[seiv] ~을 모으다, check[ʧek] 수표로 지급하다
- savings account예금,checking account 수시 입출 계좌
- bond [bɔnd] 채권, stock [stɔk] 주식, yield [ji：ld] 수익
- real estate [rí：əl][istéit] 부동산, term [tə：rm] 기간
- Treasury[tréʒəri] 재무부, bill [bil] 증권, 지폐, 법안
- de<down> + posit<put> = deposit [dipάzit] 예치금
- Treasury bill 단기 채권, certificate [sərtífikət] 증서
- Certificate of deposit (CD) 양도성 예금증서
- Money market account,MMA시장금리부 수시입출식예금

Where can I put my money aside?[3)]
High-yield savings account, Certificate of deposit (CD)
Money market account, Checking account
Treasury bills, Short-term bonds
Riskier options: Stocks, real estate and gold

---

3) 7 places to save your extra money, bankrate.com

11

lay 조심스럽게 살짝 두다

- lay 조심스럽게 살짝 두다 → 알을 낳다[1)]

- judge [dʒʌdʒ] 평가자, omelette [ɔ́məlit] 오믈렛

Although I cannot lay an egg, I am a very good judge of omelettes. - George Bernard Shaw

- lay 조심스럽게 살짝 두다 → layup 농구 슛[2)]

---

1) https://ac-illust.com/ko/clip-art/216126
2) https://ac-illust.com/ko/clip-art/2669109

- lay 조심스럽게 살짝 두다 → lay 깔다, 쌓다
- firm [fəːrm] 견고한, foundation [faundéiʃən] 기초
- brick [brik] 벽돌

A successful man is one who can lay a firm foundation with the bricks others have thrown at him. - David Brinkley

- lay 두다 + out 바깥 → (볼 수 있게) 배치하다, 설계하다
- layout 배치, incredible [inkrédəbl] 믿을 수 없는
- fort [fɔːrt] 요새, motivate [móutəvèit] 동기를 부여하다
- reward [riwɔ́ːrd] 보상하다, employee [implɔíː] 종업원
- Chester [ʧéstər] 잉글랜드 북서부 성곽 도시
- a<to> + chieve<head> = achieve [əʧíːv] 성취하다
- col<together> + lapse<slip> = collapse [kəlǽps] 붕괴

It's incredible that the layout of the centre of Chester, for instance, is still essentially that of the original Roman fort.

Start with good people, lay out the rules, communicate with your employees, motivate them and reward them.

A perfection of planned layout is achieved only by institutions on the point of collapse.

- lay 조심스럽게 살짝 두다 + off 떨어져서 → 해고하다
- recession [riséʃən] 경기침체, profit [prɔ́fit] 수익
- sacrifice[sǽkrəfàis] 희생하다 employee[èmplɔí：] 직원
- employer 고용하는 사람, employee 고용 당하는 사람
- interviewer 면접관, interviewee[ìntərvju：í：] 피면접자

If we face recession, we should not lay off employees; the company should sacrifice a profit.

Nothing kills your company's culture like layoffs.

- 조심스럽게 살짝 두다 + 옆 → lay aside 옆에 내려놓다
- confirmed[kənfə́：rmd] 확신 가진, passion[pǽʃən] 열정

It is difficult to lay aside a confirmed passion.

Prayer is the laying aside of thoughts.

- 조심스레 살짝 두다 아래 → lay down 포기하다
- turn back 되돌아 가다

You can lay down and die, or you can get up and fight, but that's it – there's no turning back.

A politician is a fellow who will lay down your life for his country. - Texas Guinan

12

come = 여기로 이동하다, go = 저기로 이동하다

- come 여기로 이동하다, go 여기 아닌 곳으로 이동하다
- 대부분, 여기 기준은 말하고 있는 나 자신이 있는 곳
- 거주하러 언제 '내가 있는 여기로 이동 come' 했나요?[1)]

When did you come here to live here?

- 모임에 내가 있을 경우, 여기로 이동하니까 come

Are you coming to the party?

- 모임에 내가 없을 경우, 여기 아닌 곳으로 이동하니까 go

Are you going to the party?

- 나 너 둘 다 있을 때는, 일이 일어나는 곳이 여기
- come 일이 일어나는 여기 공간으로 이동하세요 + in 안

Come in! 나 있는 활동 장소 여기로 이동해!

---

1) Michael Swan. 2005. Practical English Usage. Oxford. p. 109.

Can I come in? 너 있는 활동 장소 여기로 이동해도 돼?

- 같이 밥 먹는 곳도 활동 장소 여기라서 come 사용

Dinner's ready!
OK, mom. I'm coming.

- 나 너 둘 다 없는 곳은 여기가 아니어서 go 사용2)

I want to go and live in Greece.

Let's go and see Peter and Diane.

In 1577, he went to study in Rome.

- come 어떤 구체적 장소까지 도달한다는 느낌이 강함
- come 도달하다 → come true 실현되다

Happy are those who dream dreams and are ready to pay the price to make them come true.

The best way to make your dreams come true is to wake up. - Paul Valery

- come 도달하다 → come up with 생각나다, 찾아내다

---

2) Michael Swan. 2005. Practical English Usage. Oxford. p. 109.

To get a great idea, come up with lots of them.

If you’re not prepared to be wrong, you’ll never come up with anything original. - Ken Robinson

■ go 저기로 이동 away 멀리 → 가버리다

Some people are like clouds. When they go away, it's a brighter day.

The truth is that problems won't just go away.

■ go 발생하다 off 분리되다 → 알람이 울리다[3)]

■ planet[plǽnit] 행성, action[ǽkʃən] 행동
■ get dressed 옷을 입다, fake[feik] ~인 척하다

Our planet’s alarm is going off, and it is time to wake up and take action! - Leonardo DiCaprio

3) https://ac-illust.com/ko/clip-art/96504

That moment your alarm clock goes off in the morning and you don't know whether to get dressed or fake an illness.

- go 발생하다 off 분리되다 → 폭발하다4)
- atomic [ətámik] 원자력의, bomb [bam] 폭탄

The [atomic] Bomb will never go off, and I speak as an expert in explosives. - Admiral William D. Leahy

- go 발생하다 off 분리되다 → (총이) 발사되다

The gun went off accidentally.

- 떨어지다 fall → cascade [kæskéid] 폭포
- de<from> + cadent<fall> = decadent[dékədənt] 퇴폐적
- ac<to> + cident<fall> = accident[ǽksidənt]우연한 사고

---

4) https://ac-illust.com/clip-art/1075539

13

touch → take 만져서 가져가다

- 손으로 만지다 touch → take[1)]

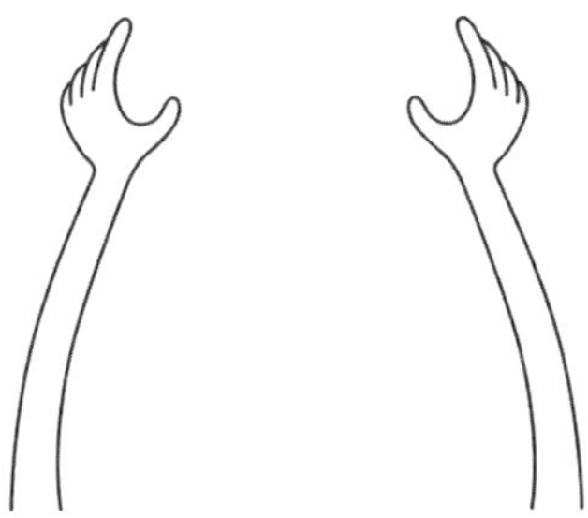

- 손으로 만지다 touch → take[2)] '허락 없이' 가져가다

Every time you go away, you take a piece of me with you. - Paul Young, Everytime you go away

The beautiful thing about learning is nobody can take it away from you. - B. B. King

- 손으로 만지다 touch → take '확' 가져가다
- take my money! 내 돈을 '확' 가져가라!

---

1) https://ac-illust.com/ko/clip-art/863247
2) https://www.etymonline.com/word/take

- broker [bróukər] 주식중개인, deal with 다루다

Too many people say to their brokers I can't deal with this. Take my money. Do what you want. That's the worst attitude you can have. - Maria Bartiromo

- take orders 충고 혹은 명령을 '확' 받아 가져가다
- ad<to> + vise<see> = advice[ədváis] 충고, order 명령

Take advice, but don't take orders. - Jim Rohn

- take someone to dinner 저녁에 '확' 초대하다
- go dutch 비용을 나누다 <네덜란드 비하에서 나온 표현>
- Dutch courage = liquid courage = 술김에 내는 용기

Thanks for taking me to dinner and suggesting we go dutch!

- touch → take '거래 느낌으로' 받아 가져가다
- give and take 주고받기, fair[fεər] 공정한

Give and take is fair play. - English proverb

Blessed are those who give without remembering and take without forgetting. - Elizabeth Bibesco

- touch ~가 손에 닿아야 한다 → take 요하다, 감당하다

It takes a long time to grow an old friend.

It takes courage to begin something, but it can take even more to end it. - Marie Forleo

- touch 손을 대다 → take 없애다, 빼다

Setting a good example for your children takes all the fun out of middle age. - William Feather

Music has healing power. It has the ability to take people out of themselves for a few hours.

- touch 만지다 → take + up 전부=~을 들다, 차지하다

And whoever does not take up his cross and follow me is not worthy of me. - Matthew 10:38

Don't let yesterday take up too much of today.

- take 빼앗다 + away 멀리 = 빼앗아 가다
- dis 없애다 + cover 가리다 = discover 발견하다

Love leaves a memory nobody can take away from you. - Danielle Campbell

When you teach a child something you take away forever his chance of discovering it for himself. - Jean Piaget

■ take + off 분리하다 = 이륙하다

When everything seems to be going against you, remember that the airplane takes off against the wind, not with it. - Henry Ford

■ take + off 분리하다 = 벗다

True friendship is a house where we can take off our masks. - Debasish Mridha

■ take off 반대 표현으로는 put on 착용하다, 입다

Put on your mask before entering!

■ 벗다 take off와는 달리, fall off = 분리되어 떨어지다

Sometimes it's not the people who change, it's the mask that falls off. - Haruki Murakami

We all fall off the wagon. It's only one day; it's not the rest of your life. Pick yourself up and go again. - Nikki Sixx

14

steal, rob

- steal [sti：l] 훔치다[1]
- steal 다음에는 대체로 도둑맞는 무엇이 나온다.

- cage [keidʒ] 새장에 가두다, set free 자유롭게 해주다
- petty thief [péti θi：f] 좀도둑, bitterness[bítərnis]괴로움

I wouldn't steal anything because stealing is wrong. If I had to, I'd steal a caged bird and set it free.

If you steal something small you are a petty thief, but if you steal millions you are a gentleman of society.
- Greek proverbs

1) https://ac-illust.com/clip-art/1686121

Do not let the bitterness steal your sweetness.

■ steal 다음에 피해 대상이 나올 수 있음. from 사용
■ wipe[waip] 닦다 + out 소진되다 = wipe out 없애다

We don't steal from the rich and give to the poor. We steal from the poor because they can't fight back - most of them - and the rich take from us because they could wipe us out in a day. - Peter S. Beagle

There's worse that people can steal from you than money. - Chuck Palahniuk

■ rob[rɔb] 다음에는 은행[2] 개인[3] 같은 피해자가 나온다.

If you want to steal money, don't rob a bank – open one. Bertolt Brecht

2) https://www.silhouette-ac.com/ko/silhouette/144364
3) https://ac-illust.com/clip-art/22276362/robbery-damage

The rich rob the poor, and the poor rob one another.

- rob ... of ...
- institution[ìnstətjúːʃən] 기관, dignity[dígnəti] 존엄성

Any man or institution that tries to rob me of my dignity will lose. - Nelson Mandela

Embrace your fear. Imagine what you're most afraid of, touch it and hold it so that you rob it of its power. - Maria Ressa

15

lend, borrow

- lender[léndər] (돈이나 물건 등고) 빌려주는 사람
- borrower[bάrouər] 빌리는 사람

○ I will lend you money.

✖ I will borrow you money.

When you lend money, don’t expect to get it back.

○ Can I borrow money? ✖ Can I lend money?

Every time you borrow money, you're robbing your future self. - Nathan W. Morris

- lend ... to ...

Just because someone will lend money to you doesn't mean you should borrow it. - Jean Chatzky

- borrow ... from ...

Today must not borrow from tomorrow.

16

stack, heap, pile

■ 차곡차곡 쌓여 있을 때는 stack[stæk][1)]

■ chip [ʧip] 작은 조각, 감자튀김 조각, 반도체 칩, 도박 칩
■ act [ækt] 행동하다, 처신하다

Risk-taking is my thing... I think of my company as my chip stack. - Jason Calacanis

Stack your money and act broke.

■ 무질서하게 쌓여 있을 때는 heap [hiːp][2)]

---

1) https://ac-illust.com/clip-art/1849992/
2) https://ac-illust.com/clip-art/1705978/

Science is built up of facts, as a house is with stones. But a collection of facts is no more a science than a heap of stones is a house.

- an<without>+archy<rule>=anarchy[ǽnərki] 무법 상태
- mon<one>+archy<rule>=monarchy[mɔ́nərki] 왕정
- olig<few>+archy<rule>=oligarchy[ɔ́ləgɑ̀ : rki] 소수독재

It is time to stop the anarchy on the Internet. We cannot allow this great technological achievement of man to be turned into an information garbage heap.

- 차곡차곡 무질서 두 가지 쌓기 다 사용 가능한 pile [pail]
- junk [dʒʌŋk] (금속, 종이, 넝마 등의) 쓰레기

I love paper. A nice thick pile of it and a pencil, and I'm content. - Cecil Balmond

To invent, you need a good imagination and a pile of junks. - Thomas Edison

저자약력

김준우

미시간주립대 사회학-도시학 박사
싱가포르국립대 박사후과정
부산발전연구원 부연구위원
전남대 사회학과 교수

저역서

『사회과학의 현대통계학』 (김영채 공저) 박영사
『즐거운 SPSS, 풀리는 통계학』 박영사
『국가와 도시』 전남대학교출판부 2008년 문화체육관광부 선정 우수학술도서
『선집으로 읽는 한국의 도시와 지역』 (안영진 공편) 박영사
『공간이론과 한국도시의 현실』 전남대학교출판부
『황금도시: 장소의 정치경제학』 전남대학교출판부
John R. Logan & Harvey L. Molotch(2007), *Urban Fortunes: The Political Economy of Place*, The University of California.
『새로운 지역격차와 새로운 처방: 철근/콘크리트에서 지역발전유발 지식서비스로』 (안영진 공저) 박영사
『서울권의 등장과 나머지의 쇠퇴』 전남대학교출판부
『미국이라는 공간: 부동산 투기· 노예제· 인종 차별 · 인디언 제거· 뺏기는 삶의 터전』 박영사
『어원+어원=영단어』 박영사

영어재미붙이기
어원과 동사

인 쇄 2022년 1월 20일
발 행 2022년 1월 25일

저 자 김준우
발행인 정성택
발행처 전남대학교출판문화원
등 록 1981. 5. 21. 제53호
주 소 61186 광주광역시 북구 용봉로 77
전 화 (062) 530-0571~2
영업부 (062) 530-0573
팩 스 (062) 530-0579
홈페이지 http://www.cnup.co.kr
이메일 cnup0571@hanmail.net

값 7,000 원

ISBN 978-89-6849-846-6 (93740)